Contents

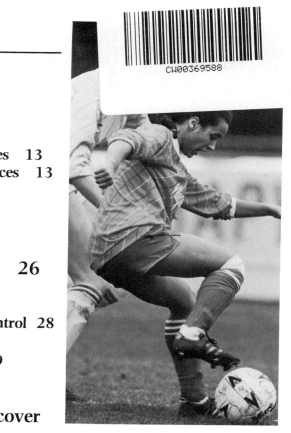

Foreword

The first edition of *Know the Game Soccer* was published in 1948. The idea of writing about the laws of the game and illustrating them with a large number of drawings to emphasise their purpose and official interpretation immediately appealed to the interest of schoolchildren, senior players and spectators. Such was the success of the experiment that a whole series of *Know the Game* books for other games and sports was then published.

This recently revised edition of the book fulfils the same purpose as its predecessors, that of providing an attractively illustrated guide to the laws of soccer; we hope it will encourage players and spectators to take an intelligent interest in the technical details of the game.

Graham Kelly
Chief Executive, The Football Association

The goalkeeper ▶ may find it helpful to wear gloves for protection and to prevent the ball slipping. *See* Appendix B on page 31 for details of the recent rulings with regard to a goalkeeper's 'control' of the ball

Note Throughout the book players are referred to individually as 'he'. This should, of course, be taken to mean 'he or she' where appropriate.

Equipment

Players' dress

The usual equipment of a player consists of jersey or shirt, shorts, socks, footwear and shin guards.

Players must ensure that their shin guards are completely covered by their stockings at all times.

While there are no specific size requirements in the laws of the game concerning shin guards, they must provide a reasonable degree of protection. They may be made of rubber, plastic, polyurethane or any similar substance.

A player should not wear anything which may cause injury to another player. He may wear spectacles at his own risk and at the discretion of the referee.

Teams should be distinguished from each other (and from the referee) by the colours they wear, whilst goalkeepers have to be recognisable as such by wearing colours different from those of the other players and the referee.

Some leagues have a compulsory ruling that the players must wear numbers on the backs of their shirts or jerseys.

If a player is found to have any item of personal equipment not conforming to the foregoing requirements, he must leave the field at the referee's request, to remedy the fault. He cannot return without first reporting to the referee, who has to satisfy himself that the player's kit is in order. The player may only enter the field at a moment when the ball has ceased to be in play.

Footwear

Footwear is an essential part of a player's equipment. Much experimentation has been carried out to produce footwear suited to individual requirements, and yet conforming to regulations. The lightweight boot, because it allows comfort and lightness of touch, is now much preferred to the heavy and more durable type.

A player is responsible for ensuring that his footwear is not dangerous to another player.

The ball

The ball must be spherical and have an outer casing of leather or another material approved by the International Board. Nothing may be used in its construction that could prove dangerous to players.

The ball must be 27–28 in (0.68–0.71 m) in circumference, and at the start of the game its weight must be 14–16 oz (396–453 g). The pressure of the ball must be equal to 0.6–1.1 Atmosphere, which equals 8.5–15.6 1b/sq in (600–1100 g/sq cm) at sea level.

Footballs with a waterproofed surface can now be obtained; this means that the weight will remain approximately the same throughout a game, even on wet and muddy grounds. A white waterproofed ball is easier to see than a dark one on winter days. The ball can only be changed during the game with the consent of the referee.

For games played by schoolchildren on pitches of a material other than grass, footballs with protected seams are available. A size 3 is large enough for juniors.

The field of play

The size of the playing field may have an important bearing on play. Because of possible difficulties in obtaining adequate playing spaces, the laws of the game allow limited variation in dimensions, but stipulate that the length must always exceed the width. Internal markings are, however, always constant. Clubs should try to obtain a field which conforms to the dimensions for international matches (maximum 130 yds × 100 yds (110 m × 75 m), minimum 100 yds × 50 yds (100 m × 64 m)).

It is in the best interests of the game to secure and maintain, by effective draining and careful upkeep, a good, level, field of grass. Where there is need for continual daily practice on a pitch, it may be advisable to lay down a porous 'all-weather' surface instead of turf.

Boundary lines

Touch lines

These are the longer boundary lines. When the ball passes wholly over them

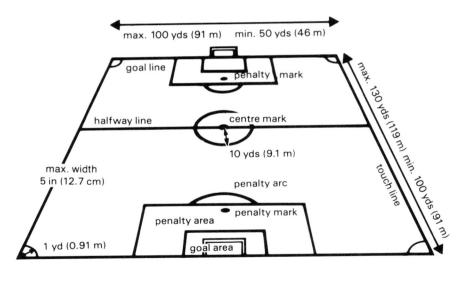

Fig.1 The field of play

it is out of play. Play is then restarted with a throw-in.

Goal lines

Goal lines are the lines at each end of the field, joining and at right angles to the touch lines. The width of a goal line must be the same as the depth of the goal posts and crossbar. When the whole of the ball passes over the goal line (except between the goalposts and under the crossbar, when a goal is scored), either on the ground or in the air, the ball is out of play and the game is restarted by:

a a goal kick (when the ball has last been played by or touched an attacking player)

b a corner kick (when the ball has last been played by or touched a defending player).

Note Touch lines and goal lines are part of the field of play, just as all markings are part of the area which they enclose.

The halfway line

This indicates a division of the field into two equal halves for the purpose of:

a the kick-off – when all the players must remain in their own half of the field until the place kick has been taken

b offside – a player cannot be offside if he is in his own half of the field at the moment the ball is played.

The centre circle

Together with the penalty arc (radius 10 yds (9.15 m) from the penalty mark), this provides a practical indication of the law that 'for all forms of free kick, whether direct or indirect, the players of the *offending* side shall be at least ten yards (9.15 m) from the ball and shall not approach within ten yards (9.15 m) until the kick has been taken'.

Note The above rule applies to offending players standing behind the ball as well as those in front of it, except in three cases:

1. For a penalty kick, all players, other than the goalkeeper and the player taking the kick, must be outside the penalty area, within the field of play, and at least 10 yards (9.15 m) from the ball at the time the kick is taken; the goalkeeper must stand on his goal line, between the goalposts.

2. At a goal kick, all attacking players must be outside the penalty area.

3. When an indirect free kick is awarded against a side in its own penalty area but less than 10 yards (9.15 m) from goal, defending players may stand on their own goal line between the goalposts; otherwise they must be not less than 10 yards (9.15 m) from the ball.

The penalty area

This is a rectangle 44 yards (40.2 m) by 18 yards (16.5 m), including the width of the lines. It serves the following purposes:

1. It indicates that part of the field in which, for any of the nine 'penal' offences (see page 13) committed intentionally by a defending player, a penalty kick is awarded.

2. It indicates the part of the field of play where the ball may be handled by the defending goalkeeper.

3. It indicates the area beyond which the ball must be kicked for it to be in play from a goal kick or from a free kick awarded to the defending side in its own penalty area.

4. When a penalty kick is awarded, it indicates the area outside which all players, other than the goalkeeper and the player taking the penalty kick, must

be, or outside which all opposing players must remain while a goal kick or free kick is taken by the defending side.

The penalty mark

For a penalty kick the ball is placed on the penalty mark, which is sited inside the penalty area at a point 12 yards (11 m) from the centre of the goal line and at a right angle to it.

The penalty arc

The penalty arc is not part of the penalty area. By being 10 yards (9.15 m) from the penalty mark and outside the penalty area, it indicates the additional area into which encroachment is not permitted when a penalty kick is being taken.

The goal area

The goal area is the area in which:
a the ball is placed for a goal kick
b the goalkeeper has special protection (he can only be charged when he is holding the ball or is obstructing an opponent).

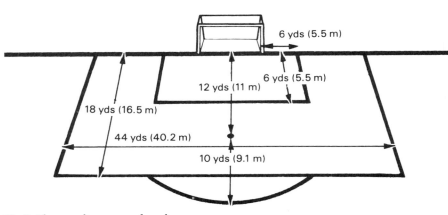

Fig.2 The penalty area and goal area

For a goal kick the ball can be placed anywhere in that half of the goal area nearer to where it crossed the goal line.

Many goalkeepers place the ball near the forward corner of the goal area, perhaps because such a position adds a few yards or metres to their kick, or allows them a convenient run (but most likely because it is the accustomed position). If the ball were placed a little away from the extreme corners, it might afford better footing at the time the kick is made.

The goals

The width and depth of the goalposts and crossbar must not exceed 5 in (0.12 m). They must be square, rectangular, round, semi-circular or elliptical in shape.

The goalposts and the crossbar may only be made of wood or metal. They must be painted white.

Whilst their use is advised, nets are not compulsory except under the rules of certain competitions. They should be properly pegged down, and so fastened to the back of the goalposts and bars that they are not hazardous to the goal-keeper. Wire mesh is not permitted, as it is dangerous to players.

Flag posts

These must be firmly fixed but not too rigid, or they may cause injury if a player collides with them. They may not be removed or inclined to assist a player who is taking a kick.

Corner flag posts must be not less than 5 ft (1.5 m) high, and must not be pointed at the top. They mark the corners, and assist the officials in deciding whether a ball passing close to the corner has gone over the touch line or the goal line.

Halfway flag posts are not essential, but if used they must be opposite the halfway line and not less than 1 yard (1 m) outside the touch line.

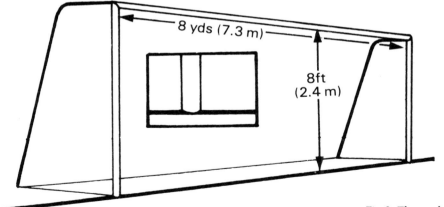

Fig. 3 The goal

8 yds (7.3 m)

8 ft (2.4 m)

The match

Start of play

It is customary for the captains of the two teams to shake hands with the referee and each other before the game starts, and then for the home captain to toss a coin, giving the visiting captain the call.

The captain winning the toss may choose:
a to kick off, or
b which goal his team will defend.
If he chooses **a**, the other captain has the choice of end. For the kick-off, the ball is placed in a stationary position on the centre mark. When the referee gives the signal, a player from the team kicking off takes a place kick.

The kick-off

Every player must remain in his own half of the field until the ball is in play. Players from the team that is not kicking off must be at least 10 yards (9.15 m) from the ball until it is in play.

The ball must be kicked into the opponents' half of the field, and must travel at least 27–28 in (0.68–0.71 m), its circumference, to be in play.

The kicker must not play the ball a second time until it has touched or been played by someone else. If he does, and the game has otherwise correctly started, an indirect free kick is awarded to the opposing side. For any other infringements of the law concerning the start of play, the place kick (kick-off) is retaken.

A goal cannot be scored direct from a place kick (kick-off). When a goal is scored, the game is restarted with a place kick by the team conceding the goal.

After half-time, ends are changed and the game is restarted by the opposite team to that which started the first half. When extra time is necessary, the captains again toss for kick-off or choice of end.

Duration of the game

The game is divided into two equal periods, each of 45 minutes' duration,

Fig.4 Correct kick-off: the players are in their own half of the field of play and the opponents are at least 10 yds (9.15 m) from the ball

unless competition rules permit a reduction in each half. The half-time period of five minutes cannot be increased without the consent of the referee.

In certain competitions the rules specify the normal time and extra time (which may be necessary in the case of a drawn game) to be played. The length of the interval between the end of normal playing time and the start of extra time is at the discretion of the referee. The referee and players must abide by these rules and regulations.

In all games a referee is empowered to:

a make allowances (at his discretion) in either half of the game for time lost through substitution, transport from the field of injured players, time-wasting or other cause

b extend time to permit a penalty kick to be properly taken.

Suspension of play

If play is stopped for an infringement of the laws, the game is started by an appropriate free kick.

In certain cases, play may be suspended for a cause not specifically mentioned in the laws. Examples are as follows:

a when play has been suspended because of injury to a player or official
b when the ball becomes lodged between two players and the situation may cause injury
c interference by a spectator or other outside agent, causing the game to be stopped
d when the ball bursts.

Provided the ball has not passed out of play immediately prior to the suspension, the referee restarts the game by dropping the ball at its position when play was suspended. The ball is in play when it touches the ground; if a player touches the ball before it reaches the ground it must be re-dropped.

Should the ball have passed out of play immediately prior to suspension, the game is restarted by the appropriate method, e.g. goal kick, throw-in, etc.

Time lost through stoppages should be kept to a minimum by players and officials.

Substitution

In league or cup games the rules of the competition may require each side to use no more than two substitutes, and to give their names to the referee before the start of the match. If the game is a 'friendly' (i.e. one not played in a competition), up to five substitutes per team may be used, provided that the agreed figure is given to the referee before the game.

During a stoppage in the game, a goalkeeper or any other player may be replaced providing the referee is informed that a substitution is to be made. If he is not informed, the referee has to caution the players who infringe this law.

The referee also cautions a player who, after the game has started, enters or re-enters the field of play to join his team without the referee's permission. Similarly, a player must be cautioned if he leaves the field of play without the referee's consent (except when he leaves in the normal course of play).

Scoring a goal

For a goal to be scored, the whole of the ball must pass over the whole of the goal line, between the posts and under the crossbar.

The ball must not be thrown, carried or propelled by the hand or arm of an attacking player, except in the case of a goalkeeper from his own penalty area.

If the crossbar has been momentarily

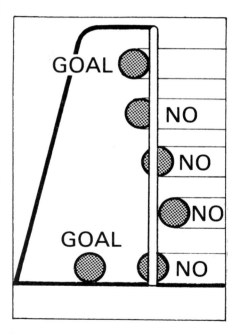

Fig.5 Scoring a goal

displaced, the referee must judge whether the ball has passed the goal line between the posts and below where the crossbar should be, and in such case allow a goal.

If a defending player handles the ball and it passes over the line into the goal, a goal is scored. Should a goal be prevented by a defending player (other than the goalkeeper) handling the ball, a direct free kick is awarded to the attacking side; or if the offence occurred in the penalty area, a penalty kick is awarded.

A goal cannot be scored from an indirect free kick unless the ball has touched or been played by a second player of either team (other than the kicker) before passing into the goal.

If, when taking an indirect free kick, a player kicks directly into his opponents' goal, a goal kick is awarded to the defending team.

If a defender taking an indirect free kick from outside his penalty area kicks into his own goal, a corner kick is awarded to the attacking team. Similarly, from a direct free kick a goal can only be scored directly against the offending side.

Ball in and out of play

The markings on the ground are within the field of play, the outer edge being the true boundary line. The ball is out of play when it has wholly crossed the goal line or touch line in the air or on the ground.

Unless the ball goes completely over the goal lines or touch lines, it is not out of play if it rebounds from the referee (or linesman) when he is in the field of play. If it rebounds into the field of play from a goalpost, crossbar or corner flag post, it is still in play.

If a ball passes out of play during its flight, but swerves or is blown so that it falls in the field of play, a throw-in, goal

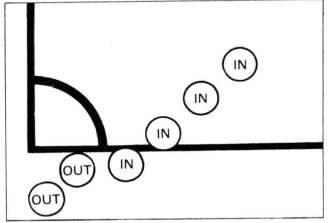

Fig.6 Examples of the ball in and out of play

kick or corner kick is given.

It is possible for the ball to be out of play when a player plays it or goalkeeper catches it, even though he is standing in the playing area. However, a player running outside the playing area may still keep the ball in play.

If a goalkeeper comes out of the penalty area and dives to handle the ball, part of his body may be on the ground outside it, although the ball is clearly in the penalty area when handled. It is the position of the ball which counts in cases such as this.

The throw-in

If the ball goes out of play by passing wholly over the touch line, either on the ground or in the air, it is thrown in *from the point where it crossed the line*.

The following points relate to the throw-in:

1. The throw-in is taken by an opponent of the player who last played or was last touched by the ball before it went out of play.
2. At the moment of delivering the ball, the thrower must face the field of play.
3. At the moment of delivering the ball,

part of each foot must be on the ground, either on or outside the touch line.

A player may raise his heels or drag his foot in making a throw. An infringement occurs if the thrower raises his heels so that part of his foot (or feet) is in the field of play without being in contact with the touch line.

4. The thrower must use both hands. It is wrong to throw in the ball with one hand, even if the other is touching or guiding the ball.
5. The thrower must deliver the ball from behind and over his head. Players can make certain that there is no doubt by taking the ball well over and behind the head, before throwing in.

It is sometimes wrongly assumed that the player must release the ball whilst his hands are over his head. In a natural throwing movement, the hands will always be in front of the vertical plane of the body when the ball is released. The throw *starts* from behind the head and there should then be a continuous movement to the point of release.

6. The ball is in play immediately it is thrown and it passes over the touch line.

Fig.7 The throw-in ▶

7. The thrower must not play the ball until it has been touched or played by another player. If he does so, an indirect free kick is taken by an opponent, from the place where the infringement occurred.

8. A goal cannot be scored direct from a throw-in.

9. A throw-in taken from any position other than the point where the ball passed over the touch line shall be considered to have been improperly thrown in.

10. If the ball is improperly thrown in, the throw-in is retaken by a player of the opposing team.

11. A player cannot be offside direct from a throw-in.

12. The ball must be thrown, not dropped.

13. If the ball touches the ground before entering the field of play, the throw must be retaken.

The goal kick

If the ball goes wholly over the goal line but not into goal, and last touched or was played by a player of the attacking side, a goal kick is awarded to the defenders. The kick is taken from within that half of the goal area nearer to the point at which the ball went out of play.

The ball is not in play until it has passed into that part of the field of play beyond the penalty area. Should it not be kicked directly beyond the limit, the kick is retaken. Players of the opposing side must remain outside the penalty area until the ball has been kicked beyond it.

A goalkeeper cannot receive the ball into his hands direct from a goal kick in order that he may thereafter kick it into play. When the ball has passed outside the penalty area, the kicker may not play the ball a second time before it has touched or been played by another player. Should he do so, an indirect free kick is awarded at the place where the infringement occurred, subject to the overriding conditions of law 13 (free kicks).

A goal cannot be scored direct from a goal kick.

To encourage a rapid restart of the game, the defender should be allowed to take the kick as soon as possible.

The corner kick

A corner kick is awarded to the attacking team when the whole of the ball, having last touched or last been played by one of the defending team, passes over the goal line either on the ground or in the air (except when it goes into the goal).

The corner kick is taken by a player of the attacking team, the ball being placed wholly within the quarter circle at the corner flag post which is nearest to the point where the ball crossed over the line.

The corner flag post must not be moved or removed for the kick to be taken.

A goal may be scored direct from a corner kick.

Players of the opposing team must not approach within 10 yards (9.15 m) of the ball until it is in play, i.e. until it has travelled the distance of its circumference.

The player taking the corner kick must not play the ball a second time until it has been touched or played by another player. Should he do so, an indirect free kick is taken by a player of

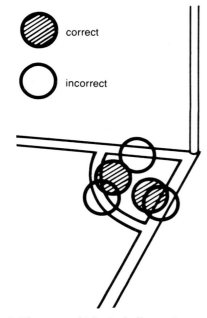

correct

incorrect

Fig.8 The corner kick: the ball must be *wholly* within the quarter circle

the opposing team from the place where the infringement occurred, subject to the overriding conditions imposed by the law on free kicks.

Offences

Direct free kick offences

There are nine specific offences for which a player is penalised by the award of a direct free kick to the opposing side. If the offence is committed in the player's own penalty area, a penalty kick is awarded to the opponents.

A direct free kick is awarded if a player intentionally:

a charges an opponent in a violent or dangerous way

b charges an opponent from behind (unless the opponent is obstructing)

c holds an opponent (see photo, page 14)

d pushes an opponent

e strikes or attempts to strike an opponent, or spits at him

f kicks or attempts to kick an opponent

g trips (i.e. throws or attempts to throw) an opponent

h jumps at an opponent

i handles the ball (except in the case of a goalkeeper who handles the ball when it is in his own penalty area).

Intentional or accidental?

Where the law states that a player shall be penalised if he intentionally commits an offence, the referee must decide whether the act was intentional or accidental.

Indirect free kick offences

Some offences are penalised by the award of an indirect free kick against the offending side. The offences are as follows:

a playing in a manner considered by the referee to be dangerous, e.g. attempting to kick the ball while it is held by the goalkeeper (see fig. 9, page 15)

b charging fairly, i.e. with the shoulder, when the ball is not within playing distance of the players concerned and they are definitely not trying to play it

c when not playing the ball, intentionally obstructing an opponent, i.e. running between the opponent and the ball, or interposing the body so as to

13

form an obstacle to the opponent
d charging the goalkeeper, except when he:

(i) is holding the ball
(ii) is obstructing an opponent
(iii) has passed outside his goal area.

In addition, an indirect free kick is awarded against a goalkeeper if:

a he takes more than four steps in any direction whilst holding, bouncing or throwing the ball in the air and catching it again, without releasing it into play

b having released the ball into play before, during or after the four steps, he touches it again with his hands before it has been touched or played by another player of the same team outside the penalty area, or by a player of the opposing team either inside or outside the penalty area

c he indulges in tactics which, in the opinion of the referee, are designed merely to hold up the game, waste time and thus give an unfair advantage to the goalkeeper's own team.

◀ A referee must judge a player's intention; intentional holding results in a direct free kick

Fig.9 The attacker is in danger of injuring the goalkeeper: indirect free kick

Fig.10 The goalkeeper does not have possession of the ball and is in his own goal area. The charge, though otherwise fair, is illegal and penalised: indirect free kick

Fig.11 Use of the elbow instead of the shoulder results in a direct free kick

Charging

Players may charge fairly when the ball is within playing distance of the players concerned and they are definitely attempting to play it, in order either to gain possession of the ball or to retain possession of it when challenged by an opponent.

A fair charge is one in which the player fairly 'shoulders' his opponent without using his arms as a means of pushing. The charge must not be violent, dangerous or from behind.

The law states that the player shall be penalised by a direct free kick against him if he intentionally charges in a violent or dangerous manner or charges an opponent from behind (unless the latter is obstructing), and by an indirect free kick if he charges fairly but at the wrong time.

If a player is deliberately obstructing he may be charged, even from behind, providing the charge is not violent or dangerous. Charging in a dangerous manner should not be confused with dangerous play. The latter is penalised by an indirect free kick.

Dangerous play is generally associated with a player attempting to kick a ball which is sufficiently high for another player to be attempting to head it at the same time. However, there are other actions which the referee may regard as dangerous, and he will penalise the player for them.

Handling

A player has 'handled the ball' if he has intentionally carried, struck or propelled it with his hand or arm.

It may be impossible for a player to avoid handling the ball, having no time to withdraw his hand or arm before the ball strikes him. Even though he may thus gain advantage, if the offence was not intentional the referee should not penalise it.

This is vitally important in the penalty area, where a player unable to beat an opponent may deliberately kick the ball directly at him, hoping to strike his hand or arm and thus (incorrectly) be awarded a penalty.

Pushing and holding

Contact sports such as soccer inevitably involve the use of hands and arms to maintain balance or for protection.

A player must in no circumstances use his hands or arms either to hold back an opponent or to push him away from the ball. This offence often occurs when the arms of players become inter-locked, and the referee must be watchful for such infringements, which may appear 'accidental'.

Even if a player is being obstructed intentionally, he may not use his hands to push away the obstructing opponent.

Tripping

The referee should be careful to distin-guish between an intentional trip and one resulting accidentally from normal play. In tackling for the ball, for exam-ple, even though the ball is played, the approaching player may be tripped unintentionally.

Tripping is not limited to the use of feet and legs. Some players throw, or try to throw, their opponents by stooping in front of them or even behind them. It is also possible for a player to pretend to be tripped in order to gain a free kick.

◀ Both players appear to be pushing each other! A referee punishes pushing only if it is intentional

Jumping

A player is penalised for intentionally jumping at an opponent. This does not mean that a player commits an offence when, in jumping to head the ball, he makes contact with an opponent. Jump-ing for the ball should not be confused with jumping at an opponent (see photo, page 18). Similarly, a player may take a leap to get near the ball without necessarily endangering his opponent.

A fair sliding tackle is not dangerous to either player, especially when clear contact is made with the ball. It should, therefore, not be penalised. Jumping with both feet at the ball when it is being played by an opponent can result in injury, and is therefore penalised.

Obstruction

An intentional act by a player to obstruct the path of an opponent to the ball, when not attempting to play the ball himself, is an offence which is penalised by an indirect free kick. The law describes the offence as: 'When not

◀ A fair jump for the ball is not an offence

17

playing the ball, intentionally obstructing an opponent, e.g. running between the opponent and the ball, or interposing the body so as to form an obstacle to the opponent'.

This offence should not be confused with the type of obstruction which is natural to the game. A player can shield the ball with his body when he is playing or attempting to play the ball (see photo on page 19). This is a feature of dribbling and close ball control.

Obstruction should also be distinguished from the personal foul (e.g. intentional pushing or intentional holding), which is penalised with a direct free kick (or a penalty kick if the offence is committed by a player in his own penalty area).

If a player obstructs an opponent, the opponent may charge him fairly from behind. In this case the referee may use the advantage law by refraining from penalising if the player successfully overcomes the obstruction.

◄ The player on the left seems to be jumping at the goalkeeper (see page 17); if the referee decides this is so, a direct free kick is awarded

Offside

In most field games in which the main purpose is to score through the opponents' goal, some restrictions are applied to prevent a player or players waiting in close proximity to the goal, ready to score from short range.

The restricting rule in football is known as the offside law, and it provides notable technical features of the game. As the punished infringement of this law results in an immediate breakdown of attack, it is essential that the issue of the law should be clearly grasped in all its details.

The law states that a player is in an offside position if he is nearer to his opponents' goal line than is the ball, unless:

a he is in his own half of the field of play, or
b he is not nearer to his opponent's goal line than at least two of his opponents.

A player in an offside position should only be declared offside and penalised for it if, at the moment the ball touches or is played by one of his team, he is, in the opinion of the referee:

a interfering with play or with an opponent, or
b seeking to gain an advantage by being in that position.

A player should not be declared offside by the referee:
a merely because he is in an offside position
b if he receives the ball directly from a goal kick, a corner kick or a throw-in

Clearly, a player who is level with the second last opponent or with the last two opponents is not in an offside position.

For an infringement of the law, an indirect free kick is taken by a player of the opposing team from the place where the infringement occurred (unless the offence is committed by a player in his opponents' goal area, in which case the free kick is taken from a point anywhere within that half of the goal area in which the offence occurred).

◀ Fair shielding of the ball, which is within playing distance (see page 18)

Examples of offside

1. **Ball touched in flight by defending player (fig.12):** Attacker 2 is clearly offside *at the moment the ball is played* by Attacker 1, and the referee should immediately signal to this effect.

A linesman should signal as soon as Attacker 1 plays the ball that Attacker 2 is offside.

2. **Two defenders near goal line (fig.13):** Attackers 2, 3 and 4 are all nearer to their opponent's goal line than the ball is; they are in potentially offside positions. At the moment Attacker 1 plays the ball, Attackers 3 and 4 *may* become offside (only one opponent between them and the defenders' goal line). Attacker 2 is onside (two opponents between him and the opponents' goal line).

3. **Corner kick, throw-in or when referee drops ball (fig.14):** Attackers 2 and 3 cannot be offside from a corner kick, i.e. when the kick is taken. If, however, the ball goes direct from the corner kick to Attacker 2 who then plays it to Attacker 3, the latter is offside. The same principle applies to a throw-in, a goal kick, or when the ball is dropped by the referee.

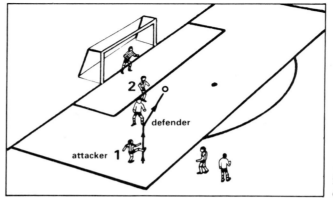

◀ Fig.12 Ball touched in flight by defending player

◀ Fig.13 Two defenders near goal line

4. Interfering with play (fig.15): Attacker 1 passes to Attacker 2. It might be argued that Attacker 3, who is in an offside position, is so far away from the play that he is not interfering. However, he may be doing so indirectly by distracting the defender from covering Attacker 2. The referee must decide quickly whether or not, in his opinion, Attacker 3 is interfering with play or the opponent.

Questions about offside

1. Attacker 1 takes a corner; it goes to Attacker 2, who shoots, but Attacker 3 deflects it into goal. What is the decision? (See fig.16, page 22.)

Attacker 2 is not offside direct from the corner kick, but Attacker 3 is offside when Attacker 2 passes the ball to him. Attacker 3 is nearer the goal line than the ball is, and has only one defender, the goalkeeper, between him and the goal line when the ball is played by Attacker 2.

2. Attacker 1, who has beaten the defender, passes to Attacker 2, who scores. What is the decision? (See fig.17, page 22.)

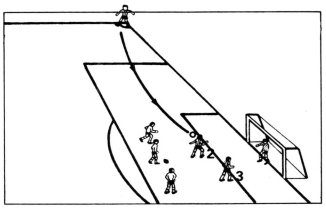

◀ Fig.14 Corner kick

◀ Fig.15 Interfering with play?

Attacker 2 is not offside when Attacker 1 plays the ball, for at this moment he is not in front of the ball. Thus a goal is awarded.

3. Attacker 1 takes a throw-in; the ball goes to Attacker 2, who passes it to Attacker 3, who scores. What is the decision? (See fig.18.)

Attacker 2 is not offside from the throw-in, and when the ball is passed to him, Attacker 3 is not nearer to the goal line than the ball is. A goal is scored.

4. Attacker 1, who has dribbled past the defender, shoots; the ball rebounds off the goalpost (A) or is fisted by the goalkeeper (B) to Attacker 2, who scores. What is the decision? (See fig.19.)

Attacker 2 is not offside from the rebound, since he is not in front of the ball when it is played by Attacker 1. Therefore it is a goal, unless the referee adjudges that Attacker 1, who is in an offside position, is interfering with play when Attacker 2 shoots.

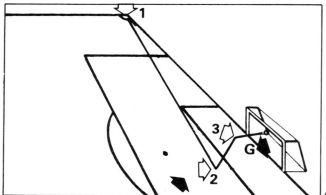

◀ Fig.16 Offside (see question 1, page 21)

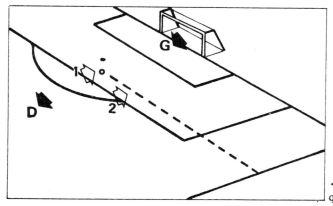

◀ Fig.17 Not offside (see question 2, pages 21–2)

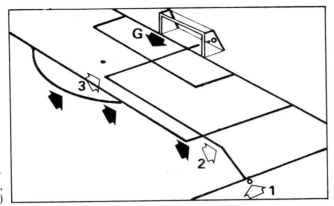

Fig.18 Not offside ▶
(see question 3,
page 22)

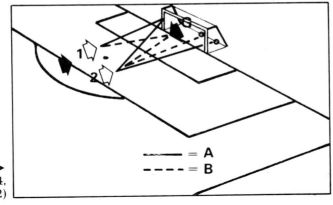

— = A
--- = B

Fig.19 Is this offside? ▶
(see question 4,
page 22)

Kicks

The free kick

There are two types of free kick:
a indirect – from which a goal cannot be scored without the ball touching or being played by another player
b direct – from which a goal can be scored direct against the offending side. Direct free kicks are awarded for the nine intentional offences listed on page 13.

Free kick inside own penalty area

All opposing players must be at least 10 yards (9.15 m) from the ball, and must remain outside the penalty area until the ball has been kicked out of the area.

The ball is in play immediately it has travelled the distance of its circumference and is beyond the penalty area. If the ball is not kicked direct into play beyond the penalty area, the kick is retaken. The goalkeeper must not receive the ball into his hands so that he can kick it into play.

23

If the free kick is to be taken in the goal area, the ball may be placed at any point within that half of the area in which the offence occurred.

Free kick outside own penalty area

This kick is taken from the place where the infringement occurred, subject to the overriding conditions imposed by the law on free kicks. All players of the offending side must be at least 10 yards (9.15 m) from the ball until it is in play.

The ball must be stationary when a free kick is taken, and is in play when it has travelled the distance of its circumference.

If, after taking a free kick, the kicker plays the ball a second time before it touches or is played by another player, his opponents are awarded an indirect free kick.

The penalty kick

A penalty kick is awarded only for one of the nine intentional offences listed on page 13, committed by a defending player in his own penalty area.

The penalty kick is taken from the

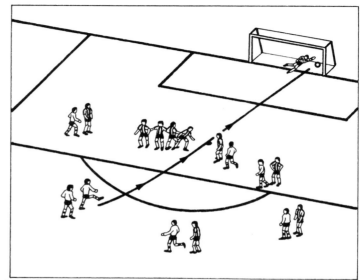

Fig.20 A direct free kick

penalty mark, 12 yards (11 m) from the mid-point of the goal line. All players, other than the goalkeeper and the player taking the kick, must be:
a on the field of play
b outside the penalty area
c at least 10 yards (9.15 m) from the ball until the kick has been taken.

The goalkeeper must stand (without moving his feet) on his goal line between the goalposts until the ball has been kicked by the player taking the penalty kick. This player must kick the ball forwards, and cannot play the ball a second time until it has touched or been played by another player. The ball is in play directly it has travelled the distance of its circumference.

A goal may be scored direct from a penalty kick; a goal is also allowed if the ball touches either or both goalposts, the crossbar, the goalkeeper or any combination of these before passing between the posts and under the crossbar.

If necessary, play is continued at half-time or full-time to allow the penalty kick to be properly taken; this also applies to either half of extra time.

Infringements at the penalty kick

For any infringement by the defending side at the taking of a penalty kick: if a goal is scored, it is allowed; if no goal is scored, the kick is retaken.

For any infringement by the attacking team, other than the player taking the kick: if a goal is scored, it must be disallowed and the kick retaken.

For any infringement by the player taking the kick, committed after the ball is in play, e.g. playing the ball a second time without it having touched or been played by another player: an opponent takes an indirect free kick from the place where the infringement occurred, subject to the overriding conditions of the law on free kicks.

Questions about the penalty kick

1. Attacker 1 is taking the kick, but before he reaches the ball, Attacker 2 runs over the 10 yard (9.15 m) penalty arc line. What is the decision?

Attacker 2 commits an offence. Therefore, if Attacker 1 kicks the ball into goal from the penalty kick, the

Fig.21 An indirect free kick

25

referee orders the kick to be retaken; if the kicker does not put the ball into goal, the kick is not retaken.

2. Attacker 1 takes the kick, but as it enters the goal, a defender runs into the penalty area. What is the decision?

Regardless of whether the defender moves before or after the ball is kicked, if it goes into the goal, a goal is scored.

3. Attacker 1 kicks the ball, which strikes the upright and rebounds to Attacker 2; he runs in and scores. What is the decision?

Attacker 2 is not offside and does not move forwards into the penalty area until Attacker 1 has taken the kick, so a goal is scored. If Attacker 1 is in front of Attacker 2 when the latter shoots, the referee might adjudge him to be interfering with play, and give him offside.

4. Additional time is being allowed for the penalty kick. Attacker 1 takes the kick, which is punched out by the goalkeeper. The same attacker follows up and kicks the ball into goal. What is the decision?

Additional time is allowed for the penalty kick only. As the goalkeeper saves the kick, the referee signals for full-time and no goal is scored.

Control of the game

The three officials responsible for the control of a game of football are:

a an appointed referee, who has primary responsibility, and who controls the game on the field of play, and
b two linesmen (one for each touch line).

The laws make no stipulation concerning the dress of the officials, but it is customary to wear kit that is clearly distinctive from that of the players, particularly in the case of socks and shirt.

Referees and linesmen are advised to consult the rules of the competition in which they officiate. The referee in particular needs to be aware of possible variations regarding appurtenances, the ball, extra time, duration of play, etc.

The referee

The referee should have two good whistles, two reliable watches, a coin, a notebook and a pencil.

On points of fact connected with play, the referee's decision is final as far as the result of the game is concerned. His authority, and the exercise of the powers granted to him by the laws of the game, commence as soon as he enters the field of play (and continue if play is temporarily suspended).

Although he may have two linesmen to assist him, the referee has the sole responsibility for enforcing the laws of the game. He must know not only the laws, but also their correct interpretation and application.

Referee's duties

There are specific duties which the referee has to perform. He must:

a enforce the laws
b reject unsuitable match equipment
c allow no unauthorised persons to enter the field of play
d keep a record of the game
e act as timekeeper, allowing for time lost through accident or any other cause
f signal for the stoppage and recommencement of the game, e.g. for an infringement of the laws or interference

The referee

by spectators

g stop play if he considers a player to be seriously injured

h compensate for time lost through the deliberate wasting of time; the transport from the field of injured players; substitution; or any other cause, e.g. temporary suspension of play due to bad weather or ground conditions

i extend time to allow a penalty kick to be properly taken

j report the postponement, abandonment or suspension of a game to the national or affiliated association concerned

k caution a player guilty of misconduct, and send him off if he persists in misconduct. The referee must suspend from further participation in the game, without previous caution, a player guilty of violent conduct, serious foul play or the use of foul or abusive language.

The referee should use the following procedure when he cautions a player:

a tell him that he is to be cautioned

b enquire his name

c referring to the player by name, plainly state that he is being cautioned (the referee must use the word 'caution')

d make it clear that if he persists in misconduct, he will be ordered from the field of play

e report the caution to the appropriate authority.

Discretionary powers

In addition to the duties listed above, the referee has a variety of discretionary powers. He must decide whether:

a the ball is to be changed during the game

b to allow a free kick to be taken quickly before encroaching opponents have withdrawn to positions at least 10 yards (9.15 m) from the ball

c a player has been tripped deliberately or accidentally

d a player who is in an offside position is interfering with play

e to allow advantage.

The linesmen

Two (neutral) linesmen are required to assist the referee, their duties being to signal to him:

a when the ball is out of play

b which team is entitled to a corner kick, goal kick or throw-in

c when a substitution is desired.

27

It is also usual for the linesmen to signal to the referee when a player commits an offside offence, and to draw the attention of the referee to physical and technical offences as well as to ungentlemanly conduct. A linesman may also give an opinion on any point on which the referee consults him.

Note that when a linesman signals to the referee, it is not an indication to cease play.

Appointed linesmen should each have a watch, a linesman's flag and a whistle (in case of emergency).

The flags, which should be of different colours, are usually provided by the home club. Experience has proved that orange-yellow and flame red are good colours for flags. The linesman should always carry his flag unfurled so that his signals will be clearly seen.

Diagonal system of control

The diagonal system of control is designed to cover the whole of the field of play by co-operative effort between the referee and the two linesmen.

The linesmen are positioned to cover

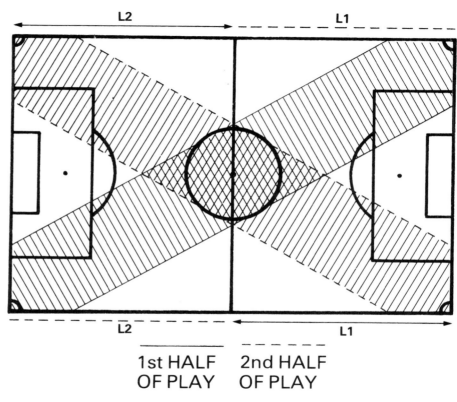

Fig.22 The diagonal system of control

each half of the field, and therefore to be up with play to judge offside offences. One aspect of the offside law involves the alignment of players, which is only accurately judged by a view of play at right angles to the touch line. Linesmen are better prepared for judging such offences if their patrol is limited to approximately half of the touch line.

In diagonal patrol, the referee moves so that if play changes rapidly from wing to wing he is covered by one of the assisting linesmen (see fig.22).

Whilst the linesmen may assist the referee, it is usual for the latter to judge all infringements of play other than the ball out of play and offside. If a referee rigidly adopts the diagonal system, he may be too far away to give an accurate assessment, or, when the atmosphere of play demands, to exercise adequate control.

It is advisable for the referee to keep reasonably close to the play at all times by using a wide diagonal zone, as shown in fig.22. This avoids the possibility of having two officials at the same spot, and also allows the referee to move sideways when the position of play demands it.

Modifications

School football

Subject to the approval of national associations, and provided the principles of the laws are maintained, their application may be modified for schoolchildren up to 16 years of age as follows:

a size of the playing area

b size, weight and material of the ball

c width between the goalposts and the height of the crossbar from the ground

d the duration of the periods of play

e the number of substitutes.

Women's football

As with schoolboys, the laws can be modified providing the principles are adhered to. The areas of modification are likely to be:

a the size, weight and material of the ball

b the duration of the periods of play.

Further modifications are permissible only with the consent of the International Board.

The Football Association

Information regarding national, regional and local courses, together with addresses of county coaching secretaries, may be obtained direct from The Football Association, 16 Lancaster Gate, London W2 3LW.

Appendices

Appendix A – misconduct

All spectators enjoy seeing fair and skilful play, unhampered by the use of dishonest tactics to deny goals. Unfortunately, some misguided players occasionally stray from the truly sporting path expected in this game and the referee must then act firmly, fairly and totally impartially to punish appropriately the misdemeanours he has identified.

Among the referee's duties has been mentioned the cautioning or dismissal of players guilty of misconduct in its various forms. The referee must caution a player if:

a he enters or re-enters the field of play to join or re-join his team after the game has commenced, or leaves the field of play during the progress of the game (except through accident) without, in either case, first having received a signal from the referee that he may do so

b he persistently infringes the laws of the game

c he shows, by word or action, dissent from any decision given by the referee

d he is guilty of ungentlemanly conduct.

In many countries, as an outward indication that a player has been cautioned, the referee holds up a yellow card. Certainly F.I.F.A. expects the card system to be used in the higher echelons of the game in any national association.

If a player is being sent from the field of play for persisting in misconduct after having received a caution or for committing one of the following offences, the referee using the card system then shows a red card.

a A player guilty of violent conduct or serious foul play must be dismissed.

b A player guilty of using foul or abusive language must also be dismissed from the field.

Violent conduct

This occurs when a player is guilty of considerable aggression or violence towards an opponent when they are not challenging for the ball. Also, if a player attacks one of his team mates, the referee, a linesman or a spectator, this is similarly classified as violent conduct. The detestable offence of spitting at other persons is also considered as violent conduct.

Serious foul play is recognised in the laws of the game as either the physical excesses of a player who uses a disproportionate and unnecessary amount of force in unfairly challenging an opponent for the ball or, in terms of the sporting spirit of the game, when a player unfairly denies his opponents an obvious goal or goal-scoring opportunity.

The latter is a very recent change brought about by decisions of the International F.A. Board, the body responsible for guarding the laws of the game and approving any changes in them. As these are very important additions to the existing and accepted interpretations of the laws, they are given in full.

Decision 15 (Law 12)

If, in the opinion of the referee, a player who is moving towards his opponents' goal with an obvious opportunity to score a goal is intentionally impeded by an opponent, through unlawful means – i.e. an offence punishable by a free kick (or a penalty kick) – thus denying the attacking player's team the aforesaid goal-scoring opportunity, the offending player shall be sent off the field of play for serious foul play in accordance with Law XII (n).

Intentionally sabotaging an obvious goal-scoring opportunity is punished, rather than merely the act of unfairly impeding an opponent.

Decision 16 (Law 12)

If, in the opinion of the referee, a player, other than the goalkeeper within his own penalty area, denies his opponents a goal, or an obvious goal-scoring opportunity, by intentionally handling the ball, he shall be sent off the field of play for serious foul play in accordance with Law XII (n).

It should be noted that the intention of Decision 16 is not to penalise every handball offence within the penalty area by sending off the offender. The essential factor is that the handling offence punished with dismissal is that deliberately intended to deny the opponent an obvious opportunity of scoring a goal. For example: a goalkeeper who denies an obvious goal-scoring opportunity by intentionally handling the ball outside his penalty area; similarly, a defender (other than the goalkeeper) who intentionally stops the ball with his hand(s), just as the ball is about to enter the goal.

Appendix B – goalkeepers

Decision 17 (Law 12)

The International F.A. Board is of the opinion that a goalkeeper, in the circumstances described in Law XII 5(a), will be considered to be 'in control of the ball' when he takes possession of the ball by touching it with any part of his hands or arms. Possession of the ball would include the goalkeeper intentionally parrying the ball, but would not include the circumstances where, in the opinion of the referee, the ball rebounds accidentally from the goalkeeper, for example after he has made a save.

The effect on the field of play of the above definition of this phrase is that if a goalkeeper, from the moment he takes control of the ball with his hand(s) or arm(s), touches it again with his hand(s) or arm(s), without it in the meantime having been touched or played by another player of his own team outside of the penalty area, or by a player of the opposing team either inside or outside the penalty area, he shall be penalised by the award of an indirect free kick to the opposing team.

It has always been accepted practice that a goalkeeper may bounce the ball on the ground and hold it again before kicking it and this remains the same. In other cases, once he has taken control of the ball as defined in Decision 17, unless he retains continuous control of the ball, it must be considered that the

31

goalkeeper has released the ball into play and the above conditions apply.

This clearer definition of when the goalkeeper is considered to have taken the ball into his control with his hands, make it easier for goalkeepers to realise what they can do and what is not permitted without punishment.

Of course, the basic law concerning the number of steps taken by the goalkeeper before incurring any punishment, remains unchanged (Law *12; 5(a)*):

If a goalkeeper, from the moment he takes control of the ball with his hands, takes more than four steps in any direction while holding, bouncing or throwing the ball in the air and catching it again, without releasing it into play, or, having released the ball into play before, during or after the four steps, he touches it again with his hands, before it has been touched or played by another player of the same team, outside of the penalty area, or by a player of the opposing team either inside or outside of the penalty area, then he will be penalised by the award of an indirect free kick.

Other books of interest from A & C Black:

Coaching Youth Soccer (Tony Waiters)
Diet in Sport (Wilf Paish)
Goalkeeping (Alex Welsh)
Skilful Soccer (Peter Treadwell)
Soccer Coaching & Team Management (Malcolm Cook)
Soccer Rules OK (Geoff Hales)
Soccer Training (Nick Whitehead & Malcolm Cook)
Sports Training Principles (Frank Dick)
Training for Peak Performance (Wilf Paish)

Acknowledgements
Photography: Associated Sports Photography (cover, pp. 14, 17, 19, 27); Action-Plus Photographic (inside front cover); Supersport Photographs (p. 1); Sporting Pictures (UK) Ltd (pp. 2, 16, 18); Mike Chittleborough (p. 32). Illustrations on pp. 4, 11, 13 and 15 by Paula Preston.